The Scarlet Libretto

For Jill —
Looking forward to meeting
you.

Dave

The Scarlet Libretto

Text for Lori Laitman's opera, *The Scarlet Letter*,
Based on the novel by Nathaniel Hawthorne

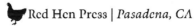

David Mason

Red Hen Press | Pasadena, CA

The Scarlet Libretto

Library of Congress Cataloging-in-Publication Data

Laitman, Lori, 1955–
[Scarlet letter. Libretto]
The scarlet libretto / David Mason.—1st ed.
p. cm.
Libretto for the opera The scarlet letter composed by Lori Laitman.
ISBN 978-1-59709-170-1
1. Operas—Librettos. I. Mason, David, 1954- lbt II. Hawthorne, Nathaniel, 1804–1864. Scarlet
letter. III. Title.
ML50.L196S33 2012
782.1'0268—dc23
2011028576

The Los Angeles County Arts Commission, the National Endowment for the Arts, and the Los
Angeles Department of Cultural Affairs partially support Red Hen Press.

First Edition
Published by Red Hen
www.redhen.org

This book is for my friend the great composer
Lori Laitman
With speechless love

PREFACE

1. THE STORY

Writing in *The New York Review of Books*, the late Alfred Kazin asked, "Why is there no opera of *The Scarlet Letter*?" His essay was later included in a new edition of Nathaniel Hawthorne's classic novel (1850), perhaps one of the most widely read and admired works of the nineteenth century. For Kazin, the operatic properties of the book were owed in part to its extraordinary structural clarity: "The novel opens on a scene, 'The Prison-Door,' that is so dramatic in its starkness that one half expects to hear the audience burst into applause."

Kazin was right about structure, wrong about music history. *Scarlet* had been turned into an opera by Walter Damrosch in 1896. But Damrosch, a composer and conductor of genuine stature, made the mistake of imposing Wagnerian ponderousness on Hawthorne. He may have missed a particularly American flavor to the story. His librettist, Hawthorne's son-in-law, the poet and journalist George Parsons Lathrop, left out a major character, Hester Prynne's illegitimate daughter, Pearl, so the story lost a key emotional complication.

Others have since adapted *The Scarlet Letter* to the stage—it is, after all, one of the most commonly assigned books for high school students in America—but I hope readers will feel that the present libretto has its own merits as verse drama. Of course, no opera libretto really has its meaning on the page, where it cries out for music and performance. But friends have convinced me that this text contains pleasures of its own, as well as in conjunction with the glorious music of composer Lori Laitman, so I have agreed to publish it in book form.

When Lori and I cast about for a story on which to base our first opera, we considered a number of modern novels, knowing the rights to them might be costly to obtain. *The Scarlet Letter* was attractive in part because we could get it for free. Re-reading the book, though, we could see immediately that Kazin was right. The prose might be rather dense for some modern readers, but the lineaments of the story were simple, clear, and charged with emotional power, as well as significant cultural implications that kept the story relevant in our time.

The opening establishes an individual, Hester, in stark contrast to her community, and we can see this in the three levels of the setting. On the ground level we have the jail, the Puritan crowd, the incongruous rose bush. High above we have the balcony where elders and ministers stand in judgment. And between them, mounted by Hester with a baby in her arms, is the scaffold, the focus of guilt and punishment. As Hester is interrogated from above, gawked at from below, we see at once how primordially strong she is for refusing to divulge her lover's name. If we know the story, we also know that her lover is one of her accusers, and some part of him might be begging to be convicted even as he fears such a revelation. Arthur Dimmesdale, the pale young minister, is in the pinch of hypocrisy, a man caught between private desires and public shame. Hester, bearing the "A" of adultery on her breast and holding an infant in her arms, is stronger than any of the men who judge her. We might add that her behavior is more in line with the teachings of Jesus than the public show of Christianity from above. Since moral and religious hypocrisy continues to be such a common story in American public life, this tale of the seventeenth century remains perennially fresh.

The novel's opening also introduces us to a third important figure, Roger Chillingworth, a doctor and practitioner of darker arts who has been away some years, living among the Indians. Hester, we eventually learn, is Chillingworth's young wife who came to the New World separately from her husband and found him gone when she arrived. Alone in the new community, thinking her husband must have died, she becomes vulnerable to new attraction. Hawthorne is rather mysterious about motives: why did this beautiful young woman marry an ugly old man? Why is Chillingworth so driven to dark arts, so prone to vengeance? Why is Dimmesdale so cowardly, refusing to take responsibility for his own actions? As the story progresses, as years pass and we see the baby Pearl become a spirited girl, these motives twist like old roots, taking violent hold of the characters. Like the Greek tragedians, Hawthorne understood that human motives are not always explicable. Sometimes character is driven by contradictory forces that resist easy diagnoses.

The town itself and its conventionally minded populace are another character. We see Hester powerfully resisting their efforts to control the wildness in her child. Hester works like a thorn of that jailhouse rose. She taunts the community by living apart from them, reminding them of the very humanity of her crime and their own lack of compassion, their inability to face up to such powerful desires. Her silence, maintained out of astonishing integrity, feels to them like an unbearable accusation.

What lies outside the circle of "civilized" life is yet another character—the vast, as yet unexplored forest of North America, and in another direction the sea these people crossed in order to arrive at their tentative purchase on a governable life. The very systems of law and belief that make possible the regulation of the town endure a challenge only Hester can fully express, as she does in the love duet of Act Two:

> This canopy of trees
> once sheltered us in love.
> Why must we suffer here?
> What must we prove?

Hester has already suffered the town's rejection, its unjust willingness to lay all of the blame for her condition on her alone. As long as she has possession of her daughter, she has nothing to lose by detaching herself from their limited vision of the possible. Dimmesdale, on the other hand, twists inside, tortured by beliefs that limit what he can allow himself to desire. Good Calvinist that he is, he feels depraved, secretly branded. Chillingworth, too, is tortured by guilt at having ruined the youth of a beautiful girl. He feels ugly and acts in ugly ways. But he is also compelled to power, which is an ugliness of its own. The most righteous player in the drama, he is a force for evil that only the truth can deflect.

What a story! With room for big choruses at the start and the finish, the story falls back into a pool of time, seen from a distance like some nagging seed at the source of ancestral American guilt. I think of the way it involves ideas of individual freedom in conflict with the thwarted and thwarting community. And the way primal religious instincts, even those associated with magic and witchcraft, are set beside a narrower and more conventional Christianity. There are big questions here about ontology and epistemology, and there is a humane awareness of passion and danger, ostracism and hypocrisy. The three major characters provide a perfect triangle of possibility and destruction abetted by an uncomprehending, uncomprehended world.

2. The Composer

Born in 1955 and educated at Yale University, Lori Laitman is one of the preeminent vocal composers in the United States—regularly compared to Ned Rorem, the great American composer known for his art songs. Gregory Berg wrote of Laitman in the *Journal of Singing* (Jan./Feb. 2010):

> One hundred years hence, when critics look back at the art songs of our era, there will be many fine composers to laud and applaud, but few will deserve higher praise than Lori Laitman . . . To paraphrase a comment once made

about the prolific Camille Saint-Saëns, Laitman seems to create great songs as easily and naturally as a tree produces apples, and one might add that hers are especially delicious and distinctive.

She has composed more than 200 art songs, two operas and an oratorio. Her music is frequently performed in the United States and abroad, and much of it is available on CD. These days art songs may in some circles be a little known form of music. Related to the *lieder* tradition in Europe, they involve setting the text of a poem— or, as Laitman has said of her own work, "My goal is to create dramatic music to express and magnify the meaning of the poem." They are a musical expression of what we find in the words, but like a film adaptation of a novel they also become wholly new works in their own right.

Gregory Berg notes, "Laitman clearly loves words and treats them with such reverent care even as she works so tirelessly to enhance them as only music can."

Over the years, Lori has set poems by canonical writers from Emily Dickinson to Richard Wilbur, as well as many lesser-known poets. She has made hauntingly beautiful song cycles and brief bursts of comedy. Poets love her settings because she is so attentive to the words. Singers love them because they stand out as performances and are clearly intended to be sung—"a simple-sounding proposition," Berg adds, "but one that defeats many modern art song composers." Many of her settings come across as mini-operas or dramatic scenes; they evolve tonally and emotionally even in a relatively brief time. Because this composer respects words and thinks both musically and dramatically, she is perfectly suited for opera. This centuries-old genre, once so popular and now verging on a true renewal, allows both composer and librettist to reach elevations of experience that might be unavailable by other means. Multiple kinds of musical and verbal art come together in the particular spectacle of an opera, and opera demands an audience, often one of exacting standards. This is especially exciting for a poet, who often writes in a beehive of anonymity.

I have never been an expert on opera, though I have enjoyed it immensely. In the 1980s, when I worked as a house painter in Upstate New York, I used to listen to Saturday afternoon broadcasts of the Metropolitan Opera. Later, as a graduate student in literature studying to pass a French exam, opera in foreign languages made a pleasant sound wall against which to concentrate. My dissertation on W. H. Auden's longer poems acquainted me with his work as a librettist, including such works as *Paul Bunyan*, *The Rake's Progress* and *The Bassarids*, and several more sophisticated friends began to educate me in the field. I have always written narrative and dramatic poetry, and must have developed a structural sense of stories over time. But collaboration with a great composer was the furthest thing from my mind when I met Lori Laitman. That meeting was an unexpected gift, requiring only our mutual assent to begin a series of rewarding collaborations.

In 2004 the West Chester University Poetry Conference, held each year for a few days in June, had commissioned three composers to set a poem of mine to music. Lori was one of them. As it happened, the poem selected was not intended for such purposes. "Swimmers on the Shore" is a lyrical and personal account of a moment in which I realized my father was descending into Alzheimer's disease. Lori's setting, performed by the marvelous baritone Randall Scarlata, was almost an opera in miniature, developing a scene of richly varied tones. It remains one of my favorites of Lori's many songs, enhancing the text with her interpretive gestures.

In the summer of 2006, Lori (along with Richard Hundley) represented the US in the Songs Across the Americas Festival, held in both South America and Conway, Arkansas, where the festival's founder, Kay Kraeft, taught at the University of Central Arkansas. One of the UCA faculty, baritone Robert Holden, performed "Swimmers on the Shore," and loved Lori's music so much that he asked her to write an opera. With the support of a new Dean, Jeffery Jarvis, Rob went ahead with plans to raise the necessary money while Lori brought me on board as librettist—an easy yes on my part—and began to cast about for a book we could use. "And soon after," Lori remembers, "I got a call from Rob saying that he had to get the grant in the next two weeks and that he needed a title/story and that in order for funding to work, the opera would have to be completed for the 2008 season."

The pressure was on. Once we had decided on *The Scarlet Letter* as the basis for our opera and I had outlined a structure—six scenes in two acts—I toyed with the sort of lyric voice that might be required and fell to work on the opening scene. Lori was soon sketching notes everywhere, including on the backs of envelopes. From there our method of collaboration was quickly established. While I forged ahead with the libretto in Colorado, Lori worked separately at her home in Maryland or her apartment in New York, building the music from my words. Periodically, sometimes daily, she would call me up, place her phone on the piano and play for me what she had composed, warning me ahead of time that she's not really a singer, so I would have to use my imagination.

This was not hard to do. Her melodies were immediately arresting, so beautiful and dramatic that I was often trembling when I hung up the phone. As she conceived the music, I was in turn inspired, moving forward with the words. Occasionally she would ask me for small alterations—repetitions of lines for emphasis, reversals of phrases, clarifications—but we never argued. I considered it a gift to hear what I had written so stunningly interpreted. We trusted each other, learned from each other, and each found the process of collaboration intoxicating. What had always been solitary for me, even deeply isolating, was now a relationship allowing both of us to grow as artists.

We have since collaborated on an oratorio, *Vedem*, which premiered in Seattle in 2010, and are at work on an opera based on my verse novel, *Ludlow*, aided by our colleague the visionary New York City Opera stage director Beth Greenberg. We maintain our separate projects as well—I can step out with other muses, Lori with other poets—but the creative team of Laitman and Mason has taken on a life of its own.

3. OPERA LANGUAGE

James Joyce, with Shakespeare and Ibsen in mind, considered dramatic art the highest calling, transcending what the epic and lyric genres could achieve. Yet opera, as Joyce well knew, exists on a highly artificial plane. "It deals in big emotion," the poet and librettist J. D. McClatchy has noted. "You have the singer belting out these words over a 100-piece orchestra to people who have had two drinks and are wearing tight-fitting clothes. How subtle can you be?"

Having studied Auden's libretti, I found him a particularly helpful model as I set out to find a voice for *Scarlet*. Readers will notice here a fair amount of meter and rhyme (or assonance), which occasionally breaks down under pressure of emotion. I did worry at times whether my tidy measures would prove limiting for Lori, but she laughed it off: "Oh that's okay, I'll just ignore them." Her musical rhythms and keys could create complex variety even in my more regular passages, and of course she could fashion resounding melodies for the chorus, the lullaby, the climactic death scene, etc.

"In song," Auden wrote with typical perversity, "poetry is expendable, syllables are not." Auden thought precisely, as always, and while he may have gone too far in some of his assertions, he was trying to keep categories in place. "A verbal art like poetry is reflective; it stops to think. Music is immediate, it goes on to become." This is, of course, why collaboration with musicians is so attractive. Poets can't help being aware not only of the strengths, but also of the limitations of their art— the earthbound properties of words. The librettist must learn how to simplify the texture of a phrase. In truth, set by a composer as skillful as Laitman, nearly any kind of poetry can be made singable. But libretti are another kind of balancing act—not just word and line, but also character and dramatic arc.

"The job of the librettist," Auden wrote, "is to furnish the composer with a plot, characters and words: of these, the least important, so far as the audience is concerned, are the words." He had a point. Opera is a composer's art more than a poet's, and song has a way of meaning what it means, being what it is, whether we catch the words or not. But experience is a matter of degrees more than absolutes, and in another sense Auden was being disingenuous. Modern audiences do want to know at least some of the words, which is why modern opera companies often use surtitles. If the script is good, we want to know it. Singers, too, feel better about eloquence than they do about dreck—though even dreck in the hands of a great composer can be made to seem sublime. Now maybe I'm the one being disingenuous; the words do matter, don't they? At least they do if we want the fullest available experience for heart, mind and ear.

Lori Laitman happens to be a composer who loves and is constantly inspired by words. My goal in writing this libretto was to distill Hawthorne's plot, illuminate his characters, and give Lori the best words I could muster to inspire musical possibilities. I wanted less to guide her inspiration than to liberate it. And I also wanted to create a compelling drama out of ideas and emotions that still grip us in the present day.

Many opera libretti fail to edify on the page. A cliché might prove as singable as a fresh metaphor, and the opera listener is not typically playing the literary critic. The emotional lineaments of the story must be lucid and immediate, and scenes must end with a hook pulling the audience into the next revelations. Hawthorne's structure was a gift, but I had to find my own language, simpler and more lyrical than his. I had to use lines in my opening that would convey the evolution of the town and its conservative ethos. So the townspeople declare there is

> One law for the sea we crossed.
> One law for the forest dark.
> One law for the savage heart.
> One law for the babe in arms.

This is the absolutist stance that underlies religious fundamentalism, and the dramatic energies of Hawthorne's story oppose it while sadly acknowledging its power. My job is not just to convey the idea, but also to provide a striking enough refrain: "One law. One law. One law. One."

When I came to the jail scene in which Chillingworth confronts his estranged wife, I had a rather more difficult job. While the older man tests and questions Hester, he must reveal aspects of his past, his vulnerability as well as his Faustian desire for power. In the face of Hester's integrity, her refusal to reveal her lover's name, Chillingworth's long-suppressed shame twists into anger and, ultimately, a sick devotion to vengeance. A lot more must go unstated, leaving interpretive room for the singers. Here I'm thinking of how much goes unexplained in the dramatic works of Chekhov, Pinter and Stoppard.

It must also be clear dramatically that Hester's primary devotion is now to her daughter, Pearl, which is why I chose to end the scene with a lullaby. Yet even this tender song can offer a thread of exposition, hinting at what their lives will be in the future—how Hester will make her living with embroidery and guard her daughter with her life.

Not having had Christian education as part of my upbringing, I had to imagine the Calvinist context of the story. A faint memory of Protestant hymns heard in the rather marginal setting of a west coast Unitarian Fellowship gave me a pattern for the choral interlude in which time passes:

> Time is vaster than the earth.
> Time is larger than our law.
> Time before all human birth
> and all we have no image for.

This secular sense of time is, I have hinted, one of Hawthorne's conceits. He tells the story at some remove, so we feel its tragedy as an old twisted root of the America we live in now. We seem unable to escape a kind of Puritanism in our national culture.

When it comes to the witch's accusatory song and Dimmesdale's guilty aria (Act One, Scene Four), well, perhaps any middle-aged man can empathize with such excoriation and self-laceration. Dimmesdale would be despicable if his agony didn't humanize him.

> O God, O God,
> the heavens seem indifferent
> to all our suffering here on earth.

> I am a man,
> a single life beneath these stars,
> a beggar on an empty road.

In opera the climaxes must come frequently, each one building on the last. Dimmesdale's isolation and despair lead to Hester's realization that, out in the forest, there is not one single law governing human life. Her bracing sense of possibility—very much present in Hawthorne—leads to the love duet in which she and the minister conclude, "Our Eden here is love." But the belief in America's meliorating properties is usually naïve. Dimmesdale cannot simply throw off his history like an old cloak. He remains checked and thwarted by his own weighty sense of sin, which he finally confesses before he dies. We have already established that this story happens in a deeper sense of time, a deeper sense of American history, so the final chorus allows for a kind of pulling back. The townspeople may not understand the implications of what they have witnessed, but they can see it as part of the human condition.

> We raise our eyes, we know not where,
> our supplication to the air.
> We must not fall into despair.
>
> Now as the light grows dim we hear
> the heartbeat of another year.
> This is our love. This is our fear.
>
> What can we do but kneel and pray,
> be kind to the neighbor, day by day,
> measure the meanest word we say.
>
> All honor to the story told.
> We understand as we grow old
> only the mystery we hold.

I hope you can see an effort to write with uncluttered eloquence in these lines, using rhyme for resonance when called for, and withholding it in more tortured passages.

The historical sense of this libretto links it to other books of mine, including *The Country I Remember* and *Ludlow*. Readers are welcome to see it as part of an idiosyncratic vision of America in verse. Still more, I hope they will seek out the music and productions in which they can hear Lori Laitman's gorgeous music.

4. ACKNOWLEDGMENTS

The University of Central Arkansas first commissioned our opera of *The Scarlet Letter* and Robert Holden performed the role of Chillingworth there with brio. All honor to him for that. George Core at *The Sewanee Review* published some of the lyrics (Winter 2011), Gregory Dowling put this Preface in *The Able Muse*, and Red Hen Press has been generous in publishing the libretto as a book. Red Hen's Kate Gale is herself a librettist, so I should mention having learned from many poet-librettists now at work, including Dana Gioia, J. D. McClatchy, Annie Finch and David Yezzi. My good friends Jonathan Lee and Herbert Beattie, both of whom know more about opera than I ever will, have given me many a beguiling lecture, Herb's punctuated with song, over lunches and dinners. On the basis of this opera and my verse novel, *Ludlow*, Jeanne Hoffman Smith and the University of Oklahoma honored me with the Thatcher Hoffman Smith "Creativity in Motion" Prize for the development of a new libretto, a fact that still leaves me speechless with gratitude.

Collaboration with Lori Laitman has been one of the great joys of my writing life, so I have dedicated this book to her. She also introduced me to Beth Greenberg, who will direct the first professional production of *Scarlet* at Denver's Ellie Caulkins Opera House in the spring of 2013. The people of that wonderful company, Opera Colorado, especially General Director Greg Carpenter and Director of Artistic Planning Brad Trexell, have given us an enthusiastic welcome and a great home for the production. My thanks go out to them all.

ACT ONE

SCENE ONE

It is June. Lights rise on a common in old Boston, a space serving as marketplace and green. On one side the hulking jailhouse where, surprisingly, a blooming rose bush thrives. Next to the jailhouse door, steps rise to a scaffold about shoulder height. Across the open space a community meeting house rises. It too has steps outside it, leading to a balcony that is significantly higher than the scaffold. With an aura of excited anticipation, townspeople gather in the space between these two edifices, most of them dressed for laboring, a few with the dark tunics and broad white collars of the seventeenth century Puritan.

A SAILOR
Over the teeming sea we sailed.
Out of the secret woods we carved
a settlement for man and God.

A FARMER
Good is the land we cleared for Him.
Free from the lash, the stranger's law.
Into the light of God we come.

SAILOR
Mark how the town has taken form.

FARMER
Mark how the will of God has farmed
from Governor to lowest worm.

The dignitaries have begun to gather on the meeting house balcony, including GOVERNOR BELLINGHAM *in his finery, the elder minister* JOHN WILSON, *and the pale young minister* ARTHUR DIMMESDALE.

GOODWIFE 1
The winter's past, the rose in bloom.
Now sunlight has dispelled the gloom
though forest shadows crowd our homes.

CHORUS
We framed the cabins of our faith.
We cleared the ways and muddy lanes.
This clarity we do embrace.

New England is our home, the shore
and forest ours for evermore.
Our Lord has opened up the door.

WILSON *(to the people)*
Repent. The world was born in sin.

BELLINGHAM
Repent. Let freedom here begin.

DIMMESDALE
Repent and hide thy shameful skin.

CHORUS
We do repent our sins to God
who gave His son in earthly blood.
We mark His law in every deed.

We built this town in praise to Thee.
In freedom know we are not free.
From Thy swift justice nothing flees.

The forest shadows crowd our homes.
Redeem the day, the rose that blooms.
The winter's past and all its harms.

HESTER PRYNNE *is led from the jailhouse by the grisly town-beadle with staff in hand. They turn to the steps, their backs to the audience, though we have just made out that* HESTER *carries a baby in her arms. Slowly they ascend the scaffold.*

CHORUS
One law for the sea we crossed.
One law for the forest dark.
One law for the savage heart.
One law for the babe in arms.

ROGER CHILLINGWORTH *has entered the crowd in the company of an Indian in feathered regalia. He looks about with deep interest at the scene, taking in the levels of balcony, scaffold and street.*

GOODWIFE 2
The Devil lives in yonder wood.
Hester Prynne is of his brood.
At night she eats his pilfered food.

GOODWIFE 3
She leveled shame upon us all
and now must wear the bitch's pall
and letter of the broken rule.

Having mounted the scaffold, HESTER *turns so that all can see the embroidered A fastened to her bodice over the heart. She stands bare-headed, beautiful and dignified, holding her baby.*

CHORUS
One law for the sea we crossed.
One law for the forest dark.
One law for the savage heart
One law for the babe in arms.

3

One law for the fallen world.
One law for eternity.
One law for the woman's child.
One law, our community.

Save us from the Evil One.
Save us till all time has run
Save us! Save us!

Winter from the world is gone.
God's light on the town has shone.
Save us! Save us!

Passionate loving One,
give us Thy blessed Son.
Save us! Save us!

CHILLINGWORTH
Who is to be saved?

SAILOR
Those born in sin.

CHILLINGWORTH
Meaning us all?

SAILOR
And her—Hester Prynne.

CHILLINGWORTH *starts at the name, looks up at the woman on the scaffold.*

FARMER
You must be a stranger, friend,
and do not know the scandal
in Master Dimmesdale's church.
Our fine young minister

now must dispel the bad
effect of this deed.

CHILLINGWORTH
Long was my journey
by land and by sea,
my bondage far off
among the heathen.
Today this Indian
kindly has brought me
out of captivity.

SAILOR
You will know the tale.
Yonder woman, Sir, was the wife
of a certain learned man
and came here ahead of him
to our New England.

FARMER
She has been here two years.

SAILOR
Misguided years, they say.

CHILLINGWORTH
A bitter thing, I see.
And who, I prithee,
might the father be?

*A gavel sounds three times from the balcony. The men hush and,
with everyone else in the crowd, look up at the dignitaries.*

WILSON
Hester. Hester Prynne,
you have acknowledged sin.

It is a vileness you have done.
We sentence you.

But in the mercy of our hearts
we spare you from the pillory
and bid you stand in shame.
We sentence you.

A short duration here
before the public eye.
But wear the letter A
upon your sinful breast
until the day you die.
We sentence you.

I call upon this man,
good Arthur Dimmesdale who
has guided well his flock,
the folk you have betrayed,
the good man you ignored,
to save you from yourself
and sentence you.

CHILLINGWORTH *(Aside)*
I know her.

DIMMESDALE
Hester. Hester Prynne.

CHILLINGWORTH
I know her.

DIMMESDALE *(looking steadily at Hester)*
Listen to my good friend
declaim your lowly sin.
I bid you speak the name:
your co-conspirator

who led you to this shame.
Your silent fellow-sufferer—
expose him to these eyes,
end his hypocrisy
whoever he may be.
Triumph over evil.
Open up your heart
to offerings of mercy.

CHILLINGWORTH
She will not speak.
Someone she protects.

DIMMESDALE
Hester. Hester Prynne.

CHILLINGWORTH
She will not speak.

WILSON
The name. Give us the name.

BELLINGHAM
Dear child, give us the name.

DIMMESDALE
Speak but his name. Relent.
Remove the scarlet letter
from your breast.

HESTER
Never.

DIMMESDALE
Hester. Hester Prynne. One name.

HESTER
It is too deeply branded here.
I cannot take the letter off,
and if I must I will endure
his agony as well as mine.

CHILLINGWORTH *(from the crowd)*
Speak, and give your child a father!

HESTER *(not seeing who has called)*
What father would you have her know?
I shall not speak the secret name.
A Heavenly Father she will know
and will require no other name.

DIMMESDALE
Wondrous generosity.
Wondrous strength of a woman's heart.
She will not speak.

CHORUS
She will not speak!

BELLINGHAM
One law for eternity.

CHILLINGWORTH
Woman, you must tell the name.

CHORUS
One law for the sea we crossed.
One law for the forest dark.
One law for the savage heart.
One law for the babe in arms.

Save us from the Evil One.
Save us till all time has run.
Save us! Save us!

Winter from the world has gone.
Somewhere with us there is one
as sinful as Hester Prynne.
Save him. Save him.

HESTER, *clutching the baby, is led down the steps and slowly into the jail.*

CHILLINGWORTH
She will not speak.

DIMMESDALE
Oh generous heart.

WILSON
Young man, it is your duty now
To cleanse the sorrow from her brow.

CHORUS *(sotto voce)*
One law. One law. One law. One.

The jailhouse door slams shut.

WILSON
Our eyes are dim. We cannot see.

DIMMESDALE
One law for eternity.

CHORUS
One law. One law. One law. One.

DIMMESDALE *stares at the empty scaffold.* CHILLINGWORTH *looks up at the dignitaries above the crowd, and takes a step toward them.*

BLACKOUT

Scene Two

Later the same day. HESTER's *room in the jail. A small bed where she tends her baby.* CHILLINGWORTH, *carrying a doctor's satchel, is shown in by the beadle.*

CHILLINGWORTH
Hester. Hester Prynne.

She recognizes him and is taken aback. The singers must convey hints of a relationship before it is openly stated.

CHILLINGWORTH
Be not afraid.
I come as a physician.
The child is ill?

HESTER
I know not how.

CHILLINGWORTH
But you know me.

HESTER
I do.
I thought you dead these two years past.

CHILLINGWORTH
And so I died. Above a year
I've sojourned with the savages,
my lot to be an honored slave
until redeemed and then set free.

Do you remember all my studies,
both medicine and alchemy?
And now my time among the heathen
has taught me secrets of the forest.

I have a potion for the child
to give her strength to bear this cross.

                    HESTER
Would you deny her innocence?

                CHILLINGWORTH
She is your child. She's none of mine.
I am a doctor, though, and sworn
to heal all human creatures born.

HESTER *allows him to administer medicine to the baby.*

                CHILLINGWORTH
Now one more potion have I made
for you whom I knew as a maid.

                    HESTER
If it were poison I might drink.

                CHILLINGWORTH
Do you not know me, Hester Prynne?
Know that I would let you live
with shame that burns upon your breast.

He touches the scarlet letter, withdraws his hand. HESTER *lowers
her head, then drains the cup of medicine he has given her.*

                CHILLINGWORTH
Now truly know me, Hester Prynne.
My eyes grown dim from candlelight,
an aging man, a mindful man,
too long a student of the night.

When I was young I dreamt of love,
the fond endearments of the flesh

as lovers fit like hand and glove,
but now my heart is burnt to ash.

I was misshapen all my life—
this crooked back, this lurching gait—
but hoped the scientific knife
could carve a more illustrious fate.

Perhaps some pretty girl would see
the beauty of my mind. None did.
This physical deformity—
my body—it was better hid.

I walked out of the dismal wood.
This settlement of Christian men
shall not know who I am for good.
I saw you on the scaffold then. . . .

HESTER
Then I have done you grievous wrong.

CHILLINGWORTH
We've done each other wrong. I too
must bear responsibility,
who plucked your budding youth away
and wedded you to my decay.

HESTER
Remember I was frank with you.

CHILLINGWORTH
My heart was large, my body old.
I longed to build a hearth, a fire.
I saw your smile was never cold.
You took my hand up without fear.

HESTER
I was so young. I never lied.
I shut the door on life and cried
some gallant man might rescue me.
I married you. You married me.

Always searching for a father,
though all men be made of clay,
I saw you in that English weather
and thought it was my dancing day.

The pattern and the mystery,
the sorrow of a love gone wrong,
this is my secret history,
this is the burden of my song.

CHILLINGWORTH
Will you never say the name,
the father of your sleeping child?
You make me wonder why I came,
only to find your heart grown cold.

You kindled life in me, but now
I am a stranger to us both.
It is his name that I must know
and I will learn it, by my troth.

HESTER
Your acts are mercy but your words,
your words interpret you as terror.

CHILLINGWORTH
Hester, do not treat me hard,
for I shall know your paramour.

Betray me not unto the town.
I bear the name of Chillingworth.

'They do not know me, who I am,
nothing of my English birth.

My name and motive are my own.
I could denounce you, cast you off.
Revenge is leaner than a bone,
but I shall have it. Do not scoff.

HESTER
A secret then, protecting me.

CHILLINGWORTH
As you protect your secret love.

HESTER	CHILLINGWORTH
Too young I was	This is my choice,
and did not know	to pry the truth
that love would come	in secret life
disguised as truth.	from out this town.
With my own hand	The letter you wear
I made the letter	will give you bad dreams.
embroidered here	Must you still wear it
over my heart.	even in sleep?
I would have died	My heart has died
but love gave me	to human love.
this sleeping child	I will possess
who is my life.	your lover's name.
I married you.	You married me.
I was too young.	I was too old.
Now sorrow reigns,	We both betrayed
no reason allows.	our wedding vows.

CHILLINGWORTH *reaches as if to touch the scarlet letter again.*

15

CHILLINGWORTH
Hester. Hester Prynne.

HESTER
No!

CHILLINGWORTH
I will have his name, his life.

HESTER
Are you a devil now,
haunting the forest?
Am I bonded to you
for all of my life?
Will you have my soul?

CHILLINGWORTH
Your soul, Hester Prynne? Your soul?
No, not yours. Not yours.

CHILLINGWORTH *picks up his satchel, nods and departs.*
HESTER, *intensely worried, cradles her child. As she sings her
lullaby to* PEARL, *she tucks her hair up under a narrow cap.*

HESTER
By medicine or alchemy
sleep on, my child, sleep on.
A daughter of adultery
adored, my child, sleep on.

You are the Pearl beyond all price.
Sleep on, my love, sleep on.
More worthy than all sacrifice,
sleep on, my Pearl, sleep on.

I'll earn our bread by handiwork,
my skilled embroidery,

and you shall grow, the daughter of
a love kept secretly.

Our prison door thrown open, love,
we shall step into light,
and though I bear the letter here
over my breaking heart,

nothing will come to harm you, Pearl,
as long as I'm alive.
This lullaby I sing to you.
May you live long and thrive.

You are my Pearl beyond all price.
Sleep on, my love, sleep on.
More worthy than all sacrifice,
sleep on, my Pearl, sleep on.

BLACKOUT

Choral Interlude: Time Passing

Let years accumulate like trees,
the drifting snows, the darkening wood.
As springtime blows across the sea
we strive to comprehend the good.

Time is vaster than the earth.
Time is larger than our law.
Time before all human birth
and all we have no image for.

The summers pass, the crops fulfilled,
the autumn harvests fill the barns.
Winter bows us to Thy will
and spring returns us to the farms.

We must devote our lives to God,
our safety in community,
His secrets never understood
though years revolve relentlessly.

Let days accumulate like trees,
the drifting snows, the darkening wood.
As summer blows across the sea
we strive to comprehend the good.

SCENE THREE

Summer, years later. The garden outside the house of GOVERNOR
BELLINGHAM. *Strolling among the blooming roses are the*
GOVERNOR, *himself, with* JOHN WILSON. *Behind them, evidently
in a separate conversation, are* ROGER CHILLINGWORTH *and*
ARTHUR DIMMESDALE, *the one looking older, the other paler,
as if ill.*

> BELLINGHAM *(to Wilson)*
> My dear Sir, I am pained to see
> the child has grown up savagely.
> Her mother proudly keeps apart
> and practices the needle's art
> to earn her bread. She's learned to scrimp.
> They say her daughter Pearl's an imp.

> WILSON
> This imp could be a child of night.
> She dresses in a cloth as bright
> as that incriminating letter
> her sinful mother has embroidered.
> Long years the congregation watched,
> observing that the child is touched
> with an uncanny spirit. Though
> we cannot fathom how, she grows
> as if unlawfully, and loves
> to dance among the apple groves
> and sings no tune we recognize
> and has much mischief in her eyes.

> BELLINGHAM
> So have I heard. I have been slow
> to act upon the rumor, though,
> because in our community
> so many troubles occupy

we few who govern. As you know
our founder Winthrop's dying now.

WILSON
And soon a new election day
will come for those who work and pray.

BELLINGHAM
Still, I have given hours of thought
to Hester Prynne, and we have got
to know as a community
if she has raised a child too free.

WILSON
We must interrogate the child?

BELLINGHAM
To see if she has grown too wild.
The mother, meanwhile, we'll observe,
discovering whether, as we've heard,
she bears a look of sorcery.
They shall be with us presently.

The two men turn aside on the garden path and continue their conversation. Meanwhile, DIMMESDALE *and* CHILLINGWORTH *can now be overheard.*

CHILLINGWORTH
Sir, you are not well.

DIMMESDALE
                    My friend,
you must not trouble over me.
I'm one who takes too much to heart
concerns of my community.

CHILLINGWORTH
Your heart is what I worry for.
The way you hold your hand across
your chest as if to stop a pain.

DIMMESDALE
It's nothing.

CHILLINGWORTH
          Nothing? Or some great loss?
David gazed upon Bathsheba,
so beautiful as she was bathing,
and lay with her, and sent her husband
into the battle to be killed.
That was the story of your sermon.
Why, I wondered, dwell upon
the guilty king of long ago?

DIMMESDALE
To make us all remember, friend,
mankind is born enslaved to sin.
Atonement is a task for all
no matter where God's Grace may fall.

BELLINGHAM
Behold, the unhappy woman has come.

WILSON
And with her a scarlet little bird.

HESTER *and her daughter,* PEARL *(wearing a red dress) enter
the garden and curtsey before the* GOVERNOR *and* MR. WILSON.
DIMMESDALE *and* CHILLINGWORTH *look on with heightened
interest, each keeping his motives to himself, the one torn by love
and guilt, the other eager to possess and to control.*

BELLINGHAM

Hester Prynne, the years have passed.
The town has seen how much this lass
has grown, and now it is our role
to fear for her immortal soul.
We charge you, speak of what you do
to teach the child the good, the true.

HESTER

The lessons that I would impart
are carried here, upon my heart.

WILSON

Woman, that is a badge of shame.

HESTER

And teaches me to lay no blame,
to judge no person but myself.

BELLINGHAM

Then we shall question this dear elf.
If you, her mother, will allow,
we'll start the examination now.

BELLINGHAM *and* WILSON *take* PEARL *aside.* HESTER, *full of concern, looks at* CHILLINGWORTH *and* DIMMESDALE, *who approach.* CHILLINGWORTH, *smiling odiously, has whispered something in* DIMMESDALE'S *ear.*

HESTER

What do you speak of? What?
What are you planning now?
Did you convince these men
to exercise their power?

DIMMESDALE

This good man is a friend

and would do you no harm.
I lean on his advice
and trust him to be true.

BELLINGHAM *and* WILSON *have been shocked by something*
PEARL *has said to them, and stagger backwards.*

WILSON
How can this be!

BELLINGHAM
The little imp!

WILSON
She has a very devilish wit.

HESTER
She is my child, a gift of God.

WILSON
We have found it very odd
she cannot say how she was made.

BELLINGHAM
She knows her letters, I would say,
perhaps the Catechism's rule.

WILSON
But treats her pastor like a fool
and answers like a fox at play.
"Who made you, little child?" I said.
And she: "Nobody made me, Sir.
My mother plucked me from a rose bush
That grew outside the prison door."

HESTER
She is my child, my gift of God.

BELLINGHAM
My poor woman, we must take her.

HESTER
No! I beg you, no! No! No!

BELLINGHAM
My poor woman, we must take her.

HESTER
Never. No, no, no!

She turns imploringly to DIMMESDALE.

Sir, please speak for me.
You are my pastor. Please!
Please speak for me.
You are my pastor. Please.
Please speak for me. Please!
You had charge of my soul.
You know me better than they.
You have such sympathy,
I beg you, speak for me.

WILSON
We'll find a proper home for her.

HESTER
I beg you, speak for me.

DIMMESDALE *(collecting himself)*
There is truth in what she says.
An awful sacredness,
a law that we must honor
lies between a mother
and a child, her own.

Our Father, the Creator,
had a hand in this.

CHILLINGWORTH *(ominously)*
You speak, my friend
with a strange earnestness.

DIMMESDALE
It is the will of God.
It is His Providence.
We must not be so bold
to send her daughter hence.

Silence. PEARL *has come forward, drawn by* DIMMESDALE'S
*words, and rests her cheek against his outstretched hand while
the others look on, amazed.* DIMMESDALE *spontaneously kisses
the child's forehead. At this,* PEARL *laughs and skips away.*

WILSON
This little baggage has bewitched you.

CHILLINGWORTH
A strange child.

DIMMESDALE
A child of God.

CHILLINGWORTH
Might we research her moods,
her personality,
and ascertain the father?

DIMMESDALE
No.

CHILLINGWORTH
But why not inquire?

HESTER
She is my child.

WILSON
She has grown wild.
She does not know
the Heavenly Father.

CHILLINGWORTH *(firmly)*
It is the earthly father
I would set out to know.

DIMMESDALE *(fearful but resigned)*
Go now, Hester Prynne.
God's will be done.

HESTER *departs with her daughter as the men stare after them.*

BLACKOUT

SCENE FOUR

A small space of light. The home of ARTHUR DIMMESDALE, *now shared with* ROGER CHILLINGWORTH. DIMMESDALE *sits in a chair, evidently ill, a blanket over his lap.* CHILLINGWORTH *shakes a vial and pours its contents into a drinking glass.*

CHILLINGWORTH
Just one more potion for you, friend.
I pray your suffering will end.

DIMMESDALE
My suffering means little now.
I seem embarked on a dark road
with only the solace of the Book
and memories of happiness.

CHILLINGWORTH *(half to himself)*
What weighs on you? What weakens you?
Is there some terror of the night
that keeps your tossing mind from rest?
Some quarrel with yourself? Some blade
of sorrow twisting in your breast?

DIMMESDALE
You watch me like a hawk.

CHILLINGWORTH
                                             A doctor
Must observe his patient well.

DIMMESDALE
You question me so closely, friend.

CHILLINGWORTH
To see your suffering at an end.
I've made a study of the mind,

its weaknesses, its inward pains.
You've been my friend for years. We've shared
these lodgings and I've seen you suffer.
I've nursed you, kept you close to me,
but fear some secret grips your soul,
weakens your body day by day,
bleeds you of desire to live.

DIMMESDALE
The way you look at me—sometimes
I fear what you would hope to find.
Forgive me. You have been a friend
and your intentions have been kind.

CHILLINGWORTH *(putting on his cape and hat)*
The truth is all I wish to know.
I am a man of truth. *The truth,*
says John, *the truth shall set you free.*
There's nothing, nothing you need fear.
Rest now. Let agitation end.
Let fever fall away, and rest.
I have an errand to perform
across the town, and I will hope
to see you in a happy mood
when you have slept and I return.

(aside)
This is the fever of a guilty man
with no suspicion of a doctor's plan
to penetrate his soul and know the truth—
the evil hid as innocence and youth.

(to DIMMESDALE*)*
Our founder, Winthrop, is on his deathbed now
and I am called to tend him at this hour.
He needs a higher physic than my own,
a doctoring of soul. Rest now, rest now.

CHILLINGWORTH *departs, carrying his medical tools.*
DIMMESDALE *drifts into a feverish sleep.*

> DIMMESDALE *(tossing in sleep)*
> What is this medicine?
> What did you give to me?
> Why do I dream this way?
> What did you say to me?
> What did you, what did you say?
> Ah!

He jolts awake, tosses the blanket aside.

> I must. I must go. I must go out
> of these confining rooms.
> I must dispel this gloom.
>
> Despair is sin
> and I must live
> to re-devote
> myself to God.
>
> My guilt will rend me from myself
> and worse—I'm torn from Thee.
> I cannot hear Thy voice!

He walks out of the light of his room and finds himself in the dim but broader light of the street. It is the green of Scene One— the scaffold and balcony visible in a ghostly way. There is a desperateness in his pacing.

> My friend. My friend must know
> I am not who I seem.
> I live a secret life,
> a man who walks a dream.

My faith was strong. Was strong!
I know it was. Then why
am I so doubtful now,
under this peaceful sky?

The houses of the town
are sleeping secretly.
Am I an evil man?
Is this some sorcery?

He changes direction in his wandering, wringing his hands, his eyes darting between heaven and earth. As he nears the scaffold, old MISTRESS HIBBONS *appears around the corner. She has a mad aspect, evidently a denizen of the night.*

MISTRESS HIBBONS
Ah!

DIMMESDALE
Good Mistress Hibbons,
out so late and so alone.

MISTRESS HIBBONS
Good Reverend Dimmesdale.
Good Mistress Hibbons.
Everyone is good.

DIMMESDALE
Have I offended you?

MISTRESS HIBBONS
You have offended Good.

DIMMESDALE
I do not know your meaning.

MISTRESS HIBBONS *(reading him)*
You do not know yourself.

DIMMESDALE
I pray you, let me pass.

MISTRESS HIBBONS
I see a secret in your eyes.
A secret bars you from yourself.
You hide.

DIMMESDALE
    Please let me pass.

MISTRESS HIBBONS
From where to where on this good night?
These are not solving stars.
These steps do not forgive.

Now she taunts him with a witch's song:

Who do you think you are?
You hide behind the cloth.
You hide behind the book.
You cannot travel far
beyond your Master's wrath
or leering harlot's look.

The hart walks in the wood,
the antler and the branch
disguising what we see.
The quail, the breath of wind,
all stirrings of this land,
remain a mystery.

In rituals at night
a dancing witch's fire

casts shadows on the boughs.
The Devil seeks a mate
to join him in the mire,
his miserable spouse.

Out where the spirit flees,
where imps and demons crawl
over the forest floor,
no pilgrim can find peace,
a wretched caterwaul
his curse forevermore.

Come to the Devil's fire.
Dance in the flames of flesh
where you and your lover tryst.
Who do you think you are?
I see you have been kissed.
You hide your dark desire
but who says the owl
and who says I—
just who do you think you are?

Throughout her song DIMMESDALE *has made gestures of denial,
all futile. At the end* MISTRESS HIBBONS *leaves him alone on his
knees in the street beneath the scaffold.*

DIMMESDALE *(in agony)*
Who, who, who do I think I am?
What have I been?
How have I lived?
If God is love—but God is not love.
If God is good—but God is beyond mere
human good.
Oh God, if you can hear,
those who cannot hear Thee,
save me! Save me!

Slowly he stands, singing a reverie of HESTER PRYNNE.

Our nights, our nights—
they were more secret than the wood
and softer than the greenest fern.

Her skin, her skin—
how could it be the evil touch
the elders taught me to avoid?

Our love, our love—
she stood before me, innocent
as Eve, stepping free of her dress,

and I, a fool,
left her to take the punishment
that should have been ours to share.

The child, the child.
I loved her and I left her there
as if my love of God were all.

I was afraid.
I worshipped the community.
I worshipped what they thought of me.

Depravity!
Worship of images, of days
that are ephemeral as flies!

Yet she was young
and came to me in loneliness
and I, a man, did not resist.

Oh God, oh God,
the heavens seem indifferent
to all our suffering here on Earth.

I am a man,
a single life beneath these stars,
a beggar on an empty road.

As he begins to regain his dignity.

Where am I now? Ah yes, the square,
the scaffold where she stood erect
and beautiful to every stare,
beyond my power to protect.

I was a coward, then as now.
Why do I fear confession so
when even scripture will allow
all men must reap the sin they sow.

He feels great pain in his chest, places his hand over his heart. A bell tolls in the distance. DIMMESDALE *acts as if it tolls for him alone. After a moment,* ROGER CHILLINGWORTH *appears, on his way home from* GOVERNOR WINTHROP'S *house.*

CHILLINGWORTH
My friend, you do not sleep.
I've come from Winthrop's deathbed—
a face more peaceful, far, than yours.

DIMMESDALE *(ill)*
I cannot sleep. I cannot sleep.

CHILLINGWORTH
The potion that I gave to you?

DIMMESDALE
I cannot sleep. I have such pains.

CHILLINGWORTH
The night air cannot do you good.
Come home with me and rest. Your heart
must need unburdening.

DIMMESDALE
But I have sinned, and I must work.
There must be some work I can do.
Beyond the town are Indians
who need a Christian minister.
Tomorrow I will go to them.

CHILLINGWORTH *(again ominously)*
But first, my friend, I'll minister
to you. Come home and rest. Come home.

DIMMESDALE, *drained and weakened, is led offstage by the older and stronger man.*

BLACKOUT

ACT TWO

SCENE ONE

Daylight. The dappled light of the forest on the edge of town. HESTER *and* PEARL, *the latter in her red dress, are walking away from town, into the woods.* CHILLINGWORTH *intercepts them.*

CHILLINGWORTH
Why do you walk so quickly, Hester Prynne?
Will you consent to speak?

Slowly HESTER *acknowledges that she cannot avoid this meeting. She sends* PEARL *off to play. During the next few minutes we see the girl playing apart from the central action of the scene.*

CHILLINGWORTH
You look at me with hatred in your eyes.

HESTER
Pity for a man so changed.
You are become a monster,
deformed by your desire
to ruin someone else.
The wisdom I once saw in you
has withered like a rotting vine.

CHILLINGWORTH
I know his name.

HESTER
What of the name?
These many years
you've lived in an abyss
of names.

CHILLINGWORTH
For justice.

HESTER
Justice!

CHILLINGWORTH
I shall reveal the man
who put this letter on your heart.

HESTER
I put the letter here myself.

CHILLINGWORTH
Not so. The man you would protect
pretends to innocence.
One word. One word from me
and he would fall
from his almighty pulpit
into the wretched prison cell,
then rise up to the gallows.

HESTER (*steeling herself*)
Have you not tortured him enough?
I'll warn him,
tell him who you truly are.

CHILLINGWORTH
And break your promise to me?

HESTER
You may call it justice.

CHILLINGWORTH (*controlling his rage*)
Nothing will help you now.
Nothing is left for me but hate.

HESTER
You cannot change the past.

CHILLINGWORTH *(with a gesture after Pearl)*
Nor you.
Hester, now be warned,
as you have scorned my love,
your paramour will fall.

CHILLINGWORTH *departs, enraged, toward the town. For a moment* HESTER *is alone.*

HESTER
How was it I once loved
a man so full of hate?
Sometimes I fear I'll burn
to death of it.
But I feel only sorrow.

This canopy of trees,
these spots of sunlight on the earth,
the light and shadow of our life—
sorrow, only sorrow.

I've heard our minister
went out before the dawn
and may return along this path.
Oh may it be the end
of sorrow.

PEARL *approaches, having fashioned a letter A out of grass. She shows it to her mother.*

My love, what have you made?
A toy of justice.
And do you know, my love,

why your mother wears
this letter on her breast?

PEARL *nods, then skips about, playing.* HESTER *walks with her, and they cross a stream about mid-stage, at an angle to the audience.*

The man you saw me speaking to
believes he knows the answer.
Our minister is seen to touch
the same place on his heart.

Just so.
The judgment of the world
descends.

But now, my love,
now is a time to play.
Run and catch the sun
before the coming fall.

PEARL *sees something that delights her and chases it offstage, leaping back across the stream as she goes.*

This canopy of trees
once sheltered us in love.
Why must we suffer here?
What must we prove?

DIMMESDALE *enters, returning toward the town. He holds a hand over his heart, pausing as if to catch his breath. He and* HESTER *notice each other at the same time.*

DIMMESDALE
Hester. Hester Prynne.

HESTER
Reverend Dimmesdale.

DIMMESDALE
I dreamed I would find you here.

HESTER
And I you.

DIMMESDALE
I've come from work among the heathen.

HESTER
Ah. And did they minister to you?

DIMMESDALE
No one can help me now.

HESTER
I would. Dear friend, I would.

They have moved slowly closer to each other, warily, keeping on the same side of the brook, each almost disbelieving the other's bodily existence.

DIMMESDALE
Hester. Have you found peace?

HESTER
Have you?

DIMMESDALE
None.

HESTER
Surely your ministry?

Surely the love of the town,
the work you do for good?

DIMMESDALE
A lie. You alone know who I am,
and all these years you would not speak my name,
you who bear so openly our sin.

HESTER
I too have kept an awful secret.
That man, that hateful man,
the doctor, Roger Chillingworth—
long years ago in England he
was not the man he is today.
He bore another name.
He was my husband.

DIMMESDALE, *stunned, slowly takes it in.*

I was so young.
I did not understand.

DIMMESDALE
I should have known
by the way he speaks to me!

HESTER
And when I feared him lost at sea,
you were my minister
and you did comfort me . . .

DIMMESDALE
These years old Chillingworth has been my friend.

HESTER
No friend. No friend.
His motive is revenge.

DIMMESDALE
As much as I deserve.
I am a ruined man.
Resolve me, Hester.
Think for me.
Tell me what to do.

He has fallen to his knees before her, bowing his head in utter shame.

HESTER
And is the world so narrow?
The borders of the town—
are they the world?
The mind—is it a wall
between us and our life?

DIMMESDALE
Hester, what is your meaning?

HESTER
Look at the forest canopy,
the stream beside us here.
What are the boundaries of the world?
Where is the law of men?

DIMMESDALE
There is a law. There is one law.

HESTER
But where? Show me
where is the world of that one law?
These trees? These portions of the sky?
Dear friend, we are outside the town,
outside the laws of men.

Into the wilderness
the spirit goes.
No one can stop it being free.
Long have I thought of this,
but seeing you now, I see.

DIMMESDALE *rises, filled with encouragement by* HESTER's *words.*

The judgment of the world,
the walls of yonder town,
the rage of Chillingworth—
cast off this pall and live.
Arthur, you can change
your name, your town, your life.
You can be someone new.

DIMMESDALE
And Hester, so might you?

HESTER
Why do we live this life
as the elders tell us to live?
Where is our freedom now
under these ancient trees?
How far does the forest go?
Where do the mountains end?

DUET:
The past is gone.
We shall know joy again.
As we loved once, under this canopy,
we shall know love again.
Our bed the earth,
our blanket sky
our Eden here.
The past is gone.

HESTER *removes her hat and shakes free her hair. She unclasps the letter at her heart. As she removes it and casts it aside,* DIMMESDALE *touches her heart.*

> Our Eden here is love.
> Throw off the stain of sin.
> This is our freedom now,
> under these ancient trees,
> clear as the flowing stream
> crossing the forest floor.
> There are no borders here,
> no secrets left to hold,
> nothing to lie about.
> Our Eden here is love.
> Our Eden here is love.

They embrace and kiss. Then DIMMESDALE *notices* PEARL *approaching from behind* HESTER, *on the other side of the stream. The girl has decked herself with wildflowers gathered in the woods. She pauses on the opposite bank of the stream.*

DIMMESDALE
The child.

HESTER
My love?

DIMMESDALE
Our child.

HESTER *(leaving the embrace)*
Our Pearl beyond all price.

DIMMESDALE
Does she know her father?

HESTER
She will. And she will love you as I do.

DIMMESDALE *steps toward the stream. He and* PEARL *face each other across the boundary of water.*

DIMMESDALE
She is so beautiful,
an elvish spirit of the forest.

To Pearl:

Child, I hold my hand to you.
Why do you not cross the stream?
Nothing should be a boundary
between us now.
Come to your father. Come.

PEARL *shakes her head. She has noticed the letter missing from her mother's breast and points at the vacancy.*

HESTER
The letter.

DIMMESDALE
'Tis nothing, girl.
Come to your father. Come.

HESTER
Where did I drop the letter?

DIMMESDALE
Why does it matter now?
Our only law is love.

HESTER
I must find the letter.

No one must know we have renewed our love.
Only beyond the town can we be free.

HESTER *finds the letter and fastens it again to her breast. She
turns to* PEARL *and sings reproachfully.*

Now do you know your mother, child?
Now do you know me?

PEARL *leaps across the brook, dashes past* DIMMESDALE *and
into her mother's arms. The minister, chastened by this turn of
events, looks on.*

DIMMESDALE
She has her mother now.

HESTER
Also her father.

DIMMESDALE
So I would hope to be. But how?

HESTER *lets* PEARL *run off again. Pearl stays by the stream,
casting her gathered flowers on the water.*

HESTER *(firming a plan)*
There is a ship in Boston harbor
bound for far away,
and we could book our passage, love,
after Election Day.

DIMMESDALE
I've met the Captain on the street,
given a sailor's prayer.
He's bound for far away, my love.
We'll find our freedom there.

DUET:
The pattern and the mystery
brought us together here.
We shall abandon history,
live where the weather's fair.

Under the forest canopy
we shall discover now
out in the world we can be free.
This is our perfect vow.

HESTER
The past is gone.

DIMMESDALE
The future's ours.

HESTER
There is a ship.

DIMMESDALE
Election Day.

HESTER
Prepare, my love.

DIMMESDALE
Prepare and pray.

HESTER
I'll pray for us.

DIMMESDALE
I'll pray for us.

HESTER
Farewell.

DIMMESDALE
Farewell.

They kiss. PEARL *runs to her mother, and they exit toward the town, hand in hand.*

Farewell.

DIMMESDALE *watches them go, then suddenly feels a pain in his chest and places his hand there. He nods, as if recognizing an old truth.*

> My happiness departs.
> The stream runs clear, but I
> am darkening like the sky
> above these trees.
>
> Who do I think I am?
> Have I forsaken God?
> How can I face the town?
> Who, says the owl. Who?

He paces, increasingly anxious, looking offstage where HESTER *has gone.*

> Hester, I am not strong like you.
> Hester, I'll not live long like you.
> Shall I create a life with you?
> Free of the prying eyes with you?
> Sail with you far away, my love,
> under the perfect sky above?

He raises his eyes to the canopy of trees.

> Hester. Hester Prynne.
> Can we be free of sin?

BLACKOUT

48

Scene Two

In the darkness between the final two scenes we can hear the chorus chanting:

One law for the fallen world.
One law for eternity.
One law for the woman's child.
One law, our community.

Save us from the Evil One.
Give us Thy blessed Son.
Save us, save us!

One law, our community.
One law, our community.

One law. One law. One law. One.

Lights rise on the street as we saw it at the beginning of the opera: meeting house, scaffold, jail, all decorated for Election Day. The crowd is gathering: farmers, fishermen, sailors, goodwives, a few Indians.

Strike up the march. Let music play.
Election Day! Election Day!

FARMER
Today the people have a say.

CHORUS
Election Day! Election Day!

SAILOR
From houses crowding to the bay,

GOODWIFE 1
From forests dark as ebony,

GOODWIFE 2
The people come to work and pray.

GOODWIFE 3
We worship in community.

CHORUS
Election Day! Election Day!

At one fringe of the crowd we have noticed old CHILLINGWORTH
conferring with a SHIPMASTER, *their conversation apparently
full of dark plotting. At another end* HESTER *and* PEARL *have
arrived.* HESTER's *plain dress is adorned with the scarlet letter.*
PEARL *wears her brighter, bolder attire.* HESTER *is watching
the crowd, evidently looking for* DIMMESDALE. *Instead, the*
SHIPMASTER, *released from* CHILLINGWORTH, *accosts her.*

SHIPMASTER
A word, a word!

HESTER
You have a berth for us?

SHIPMASTER
Madam, I do. For you, your child,
and the gentleman you mentioned.

HESTER
We're bound away from here.

SHIPMASTER
That is the wish of others, too.
The old man, Chillingworth, has asked

if he might sail with us, and I
have offered him a berth near yours.

Before HESTER *can react,* MISTRESS HIBBONS *emerges from the crowd. Now* HESTER'S *attention is distracted from two sides at once.*

HESTER
This cannot be!

MISTRESS HIBBONS
Who do you look for? Who?
Is it the minister
who met you in the wood?

SHIPMASTER
We'll take the tide and sail
before the week is out.

MISTRESS HIBBONS
A woman knows the world,
the secrets of the wood,
and you cannot escape.
I know you are not good.

HESTER
Madame, you mistake me.

SHIPMASTER
We'll take the tide and sail.

MISTRESS HIBBONS
I see you've brought your girl.

To Pearl:

> Thou art the lineage
> of the Prince of the Air!
> Wilt thou fly with me some night
> to meet the minister?

PEARL *looks desperately at her mother, who fends off the old woman. Just at that moment a drum roll sounds the start of the parade.* MISTRESS HIBBONS, *startled, melts into the crowd, later to leave the stage altogether. From behind the meeting house a procession emerges to music that sounds both martial and religious. Flags and banners wave. At the head of the procession are* DIMMESDALE, *looking pale and profoundly distracted,* WILSON *and* BELLINGHAM.

> SHIPMASTER *(departing)*
> We sail within the week.

CHILLINGWORTH *has fallen in behind the leaders with a kind of eager piety masking his dark intent. Most of the crowd joins the parade as it progresses. A few, like* HESTER *and* PEARL, *remain as bystanders. The march circles the stage, passing the scaffold, crossing to the meeting house steps, which the three dignitaries mount as the chorus sings.*

> CHORUS
> Strike up the march. Let the music play.
> Today the people have their say.
> Bless, O Lord, Election Day,
> and all of us who work and pray.
> Election Day! Election Day!
>
> God names His own elect to stay.
> We have a voice, who work and pray.
> It is our Lord who offers grace
> and not the humble human race.

We have a voice, who work and pray.
Election Day! Election Day!

BELLINGHAM *(calling for order)*
Hear ye, hear ye, one and all,
to mark our celebration now
acknowledging our God, we bow
our heads before this meeting hall.

WILSON *(praying)*
Come Holy Ghost, Creator blest,
vouchsafe within our hearts to rest;
come with Thy grace and heavenly aid,
and fill the hearts which Thou hast made.

ALL
Amen.

BELLINGHAM *(indicating Dimmesdale)*
Our hearts are filled, and now we pause
to listen to our shepherd here
who knows his flock and knows the laws
that bind us in this earthly sphere.

DIMMESDALE *has been standing with head bowed, a hand over his heart. He now lifts his head slowly, looks over the crowd below, unable to see* HESTER *and* PEARL. *When he begins his sermon it is slowly, hesitantly, then gaining in strength, making his last vital gestures.*

DIMMESDALE
Dear friends. Dear brethren gathered here
on this our proud Election Day
our settlement has cause to cheer,
and I have only this to say:
The forest far beyond our farms
now echoes with our industry.

Risking a plenitude of harms,
our fishermen patrol the sea,

but what are we? Yea, who are we
who toil and pray and clear the land?
We are the Lord's community,
His grace delivered at His hand.

Free in our choices, honor bound
to turn the Devil off the path,
we consecrate our bit of ground
and bow our heads before the Truth.

Community! Community
has always helped us to endure.
In freedom know we are not free
unless our pilgrim hearts be pure.

In the last verse his mind begins to reel at what he is saying.

CHORUS
Community! Community
has always helped us to endure.
In freedom know we are not free
unless our pilgrim hearts be pure.

DIMMESDALE
This still small voice, the wilderness
around us darkened by our terror—
come Holy Ghost, Creator blest
and guide us out of sin and error.

CHORUS
In freedom know we are not free
unless our pilgrim hearts be pure.

As the chorus continues, the dignitaries descend from the meeting house balcony to the street, rejoining the procession.

It is our God who offers grace
and not the humble human race.
We have a choice. We work and pray.
Election Day. Election Day.

One law for the forest dark.
One law for the sea we crossed.
One law for the savage heart.
One law for the saved, the lost.

As he descends the steps, Dimmesdale *has been looking into the crowd. His physical weakness is now so apparent that* Wilson *offers him support. Suddenly before the scaffold steps the crowd parts, revealing* Hester, *who holds* Pearl *by the hand.* Dimmesdale *pauses, seeing this, then reaches out toward them.*

DIMMESDALE
Hester. Hester!

The crowd has silenced, focusing only on this small family facing each other in public before the scaffold steps.

Come hither, Pearl.
You are my Pearl beyond all price.

Roger Chillingworth, *who has stood by in the crowd, pushes forward, taking* Dimmesdale *by the arm and forcing him away.*

CHILLINGWORTH
Wave back that woman!
Cast off this child
and do not blacken
your name with dishonor.

DIMMESDALE
Tempter. Tempter!
Thou art the Devil,
but with God's help
I shall escape you.

Turning to Hester and Pearl.

Hester. Hester Prynne.
Give me your strength.
Let it be guided by God.
Let us join hands
and banish the lie.
Come, Hester, come!
Give me your arm.

CHILLINGWORTH
Wave back that woman.
She is the Devil's mate.
Witness the letter
she bears on her breast!

DIMMESDALE *(to Hester)*
Give me your arm.

HESTER *helps* DIMMESDALE *as he mounts the scaffold.* PEARL
joins them, taking her father's other arm.

CHILLINGWORTH
What is this foolishness?
You think it bravery?
Now you would spit in the face
of your truest friend?
What is my wrath to you now?
No spot on this earth

would be safe from my spite
except for this scaffold.

Atop the scaffold, DIMMESDALE *looks* HESTER *in the eye. They
have in this brief moment, despite the awestruck crowd below
them, a space of intimacy.*

DIMMESDALE *(weakly)*
Is this not better, Hester Prynne,
than our dreams in the forest?

HESTER
I know not, Arthur. I know not.

DIMMESDALE
For you and Pearl, the truth at last,
and pray that God is merciful.
Hester, I am a dying man.
I should make haste to meet the truth.

DIMMESDALE *turns to face the crowd.*

Ye people of New England, hear!
At last I stand upon the spot
I should have taken years ago.
I should have stood beside this woman.
She is no Pharisee. She makes
no false display of piety,
but bears the letter of our sin,
our common sin, without complaint.

You judged her and I let you judge,
and I stood by among you there,
as much a sinner, a secret man,
equal in infamy, afraid
of what community would say.

He steps forward.

> God saw the letter on her heart
> and saw . . . He saw the sin in me.
> The Devil plied his wicked power,
> leaving me afraid. No more!
> Behold. Behold!

DIMMESDALE *tears open his robe and tunic, revealing a scarlet letter A as if branded upon his chest. No sooner has he displayed the mark to the astonished crowd than he collapses on the scaffold.* HESTER *and* PEARL *come to his aid.*

>   CHILLINGWORTH
> You have escaped me.
> You have escaped me!

>   DIMMESDALE
> May God forgive you,
> and may you learn the ways
> you too have sinned.

>   CHILLINGWORTH
> You have escaped me.

DIMMESDALE'S *eyes are now fixed on his family.* HESTER *holds his head on her lap.*

>   DIMMESDALE *(weakening)*
> My Pearl, you see
> your father before you.
> This is no forest dream,
> but will you kiss me now?

PEARL *kisses her father and begins to weep.*

> Hester. Hester Prynne.

HESTER
My love, shall we not have
immortal life?
Have we not suffered enough?

DIMMESDALE
I bear the mark.
It is God's will.
We have the truth.
Praised be His name.
And now, perhaps, the peace
that passeth understanding . . .

DIMMESDALE *dies.* HESTER *wails and bows her head over his body. In the crowd below everyone bows heads except* CHILLINGWORTH, *who stands apart in his impotent rage. Slowly men from the crowd mount the scaffold to the body. When* HESTER *can acknowledge them, she stands back,* PEARL *beside her, while men lift* DIMMESDALE'S *body. They carry it slowly and carefully down the steps, then off the stage, a parade of mourners now. For the remainder of the opera we seem to move into abstracted space—a dream time in which the whole of history can be glimpsed.*

CHORUS
Let days accumulate like trees,
the driven rain, the darkening wood.
As summer blows across the sea
we strive to comprehend the good.

Time is vaster than the earth.
Time is larger than our law.
Time before all human birth
and all we have no image for.

SAILOR
Who is the man they bury here?
Why do the women weep so loud?

GOODWIFE 1
He was the minister we loved,
caught in the nets of his desire.

GOODWIFE 2
How will the town remember him?
What is a name upon a stone?

FARMER
Only as one who labored here,
part of the harvest we have made.

CHORUS
We must devote our lives to God,
our safety in community,
His secrets never understood
though years revolve relentlessly.

CHILLINGWORTH
What will become of men who hate?
How will they end their pilgrimage?

WILSON
They are the vine without a fruit,
withering slowly into death.
Hatred's voice will not survive
as long as we have love to give.

CHILLINGWORTH
Alas!

He seems to shrink off stage. By now the men who carried DIMMESDALE *off have rejoined the chorus.*

HESTER
What will become of those who love?
How can they live where they are judged?

BELLINGHAM
There is a story, Hester Prynne,
one to be told down all the years.

GOODWIFE 3
A Pearl beyond all price will grow
across the sea and far away.
Her mother disappeared with her,
knowing she'd return one day.

FARMER
Return to find a grave beside
the secret father of her child.
Their single stone, if you should seek it,
is wound about with ivy wild.

HESTER
Alas!

SAILOR
And some will say across the sea
a lovely woman sailed for home.
Adorned with riches, married now,
to old New England she has come.

GOODWIFE 1
She walks beside the bay
out where the cottage stood,
puts flowers on the grave,
and wanders in the wood.

HESTER
She is the Pearl beyond all price,

the heiress of the secret heart,
the dream of freedom realized,
still practicing her mother's art.
She is the reason I have lived!
The people see her walk alone,
how proudly now she has survived.
She kneels beside her mother's stone.

CHORUS
The seasons toll like passing bells.
The harbor grows, the nation moves
beyond the farthest of the hills.

HESTER AND PEARL
Alas!

CHORUS
Alas!

BELLINGHAM
And on the grave, some people say,
a scarlet letter can be seen
on a sable field—the letter A!

FARMER
Alas, how time obscures the tale.
The seasons toll like passing bells.
The mountains fill with snow, the wood
is darkening. It seems to brood.

WILSON
This is the mind of God, they say,
light of the stars that shine at night,
flight of the hawk across the day,
tears of the lonely acolyte.

CHORUS

We raise our eyes, we know not where,
our supplication to the air.
We must not fall into despair.

Now as the light grows dim we hear
the heartbeat of another year.
This is our love. This is our fear.

What can we do but kneel and pray,
be kind to our neighbor, day by day,
measure the meanest word we say.

All honor to the story told.
We understand as we grow old
only the mystery we hold.

BLACKOUT

BIOGRAPHICAL NOTE

David Mason is the Poet Laureate of Colorado. His books of poems include *The Buried Houses* (winner of the Nicholas Roerich Poetry Prize), *The Country I Remember* (winner of the Alice Fay Di Castagnola Award), and *Arrivals*. His verse-novel, *Ludlow*, won the Colorado Book Award in 2007, and was named Best Poetry Book of the year by the *Contemporary Poetry Review* and the National Cowboy and Western Heritage Museum. It was also featured on the *PBS NewsHour*. Mason is the author of an essay collection, *The Poetry of Life and the Life of Poetry*, and a memoir, *News from the Village*, which appeared in 2010. A new collection of essays, *Two Minds of a Western Poet*, followed in 2011. He recently won the Thatcher Hoffman Smith Creativity in Motion Prize for the development of a new libretto. A former Fulbright fellow to Greece, he teaches at Colorado College.